Ribbons, Buttons & Beads

Ribbons, Buttons & Beads

projects
for a
romantic home

Mary Jo Hiney

Sterling Publishing Co., Inc. New York
A Sterling/Chapelle Book

Chapelle, Ltd.:
  Jo Packham
  Sara Toliver
  Cindy Stoeckl

Editor: Lecia Monsen
Art Director: Karla Haberstich
Graphic Illustrator: Kim Taylor
Copy Editor: Marilyn Goff

Staff: Kelly Ashkettle, Areta Bingham, Donna Chambers, Ray Cornia, Emily Frandsen, Marilyn Goff, Lana Hall, Susan Jorgensen, Barbara Milburn, Suzy Skadburg, Desirée Wybrow

If you have any questions or comments, please contact:
Chapelle, Ltd., Inc., P.O. Box 9252, Ogden, UT 84409
  (801) 621-2777 • (801) 621-2788 Fax
  e-mail: chapelle@chapelleltd.com
  web site: www.chapelleltd.com

Library of Congress Cataloging-in-Publication Data

Hiney, Mary Jo.
  Ribbons, buttons, & beads : projects for a romantic home / Mary Jo Hiney.
      p. cm.
  "A Sterling/Chapelle book."
  ISBN 1-40270-388-0
  1. Textile crafts. 2. Interior decoration. 3. House furnishings. I. Title: Ribbons, buttons, and beads. II. Title.
TT699 .H56 2003
746--dc21
                                    2003009347

10 9 8 7 6 5 4 3 2 1

Published by Sterling Publishing Co., Inc.
387 Park Avenue South, New York, NY 10016
©2003 by Mary Jo Hiney
Distributed in Canada by Sterling Publishing
c/o Canadian Manda Group, One Atlantic Avenue, Suite 105
Toronto, Ontario, Canada M6K 3E7
Distributed in Great Britain by Chrysalis Books
64 Brewery Road, London N7 9NT, England
Distributed in Australia by Capricorn Link (Australia) Pty. Ltd.
P. O. Box 704, Windsor, NSW 2756, Australia
Printed in China
All Rights Reserved

Sterling ISBN 1-4027-0388-0

Introduction

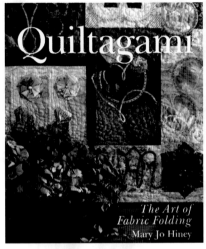

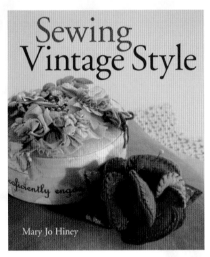

Enjoy these other Mary Jo Hiney books.

Mary Jo Hiney works as a freelance author, designer, and project contributor in the fabric and craft industry, gladly sharing skill-filled secrets gathered over a lifetime of experience.

Hiney's designs focus on gifts and decorative accessories. Her one-of-a-kind pieces display beauty enhanced with function.

Hiney is also the author of *The Beaded Object, Romantic Silk Ribbon Keepsakes, Two-Hour Vests, Beautiful Foundation-Pieced Quilt Blocks, Creating with Lace,* and *Fabulous Fabric Embellishments.*

This year, everything that was is different. For my family, Evan, Josh, Lexi and Claire.

Contents

MATERIALS *(For one box)*

Accent button or vintage floral spray

Assorted ribbons, trims, or laces

Box: die-cut

Decorative tissue paper

TOOLS

Bone folder   Large paper bag

Craft scissors   Spray adhesive

Darning needle   Utility knife

Glue stick

HOW TO MAKE BOXES

1. Cover the work surface with paper bag.

2. Score lines on inside of die-cut, using bone folder.

3. Apply a light coat of spray adhesive to one side of die-cut.

4. Adhere tissue paper smoothly onto die-cut. Repeat for other side.

5. Trim excess tissue from edges of die-cut. Recut flaps and slashes, using utility knife.

6. Fold box on scored lines and, using glue stick, glue together.

7. Using glue stick, decorate box with ribbons, trims, or floral sprays.

8. Fill box. Using darning needle and ribbon, stitch flap onto box front. Slip ribbon through button before tying into a bow.

Pretty Party Favor Boxes

Customize your guest party favors for special keepsake memories. At each place setting, serve up a beribboned slice of paper-box pie or a spot of fancy paper-box tea. Tuck in a wish.

MATERIALS

(For 4"-diameter clock face)

Beaded-fringe tape: crystal (¼ yd)

Beads:

    11/0, seed, crystal, silver-lined

    ⅝", teardrop, crystal (2)

Matching thread

Metal clock: aged white

Ribbons:

    1", satin, white (4")

    7mm, silk, gray (18"); white (4 yds)

TOOLS

E6000 adhesive

Needles:

    size 3, embroidery

    hand-sewing

Pencil

Tape measure

Timeless Timepiece

Make a period bedroom timeless. Purchase a fanciful clock in any unique shape and trim the face with ribbon flowers and vintage beads.

HOW TO EMBELLISH THE FRAME

1. Adhere beaded-fringe tape around clock face. *Note: If the tape on which the beads have been stitched to is too wide to fit around the clock face, fold the tape in half or thirds, as necessary. Hand-stitch or glue the folded tape to make more manageable.*

Make Fuchsia Flower

2. Thread the hand-sewing needle with 6" thread length.

3. To form a fuchsia, fold 4" length of satin ribbon in half and crease center. Fold back one raw end of ribbon ¼". Fold remaining raw end of ribbon back so it overlaps center crease ¼". Fold first folded end of ribbon back to meet center crease. See (1).

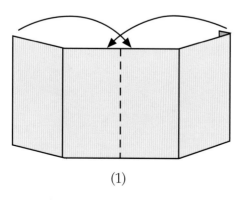

(1)

4. Center and pull threaded needle through ¼" "seam" from back to front side for stem. Mark a diamond shape on fuchsia. See (2). Hand-stitch along mark. Tightly pull thread to gather, then secure thread. Completed Fuchsia. See (3).

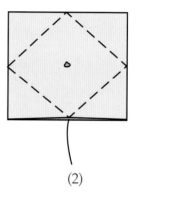

(2)

(3)

Make Rosette

5. Cut 7mm ribbons into 9" lengths.

6. Fold one 9" length of ribbon down at right angle, creating a post to hold onto. See (1).

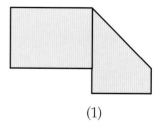

(1)

12

7. Fold post in half lengthwise and roll between fingers in direction of fold to end of right-angle fold. Stitch in place securely with thread. See (2).

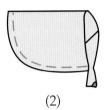

(2)

8. Continue folding and rolling ribbon. Stitch to secure.

9. When ribbon is rolled and folded half its length, hand-stitch a gathering stitch along the bottom edge of remaining length of ribbon. Taper stitches at ribbon end. See (3).

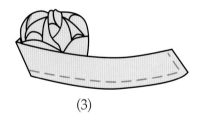

(3)

10. Tightly pull gathering stitch and wrap gathered section around folded rose. Stitch in place to secure. Completed Rosette. See (4).

(4)

11. Stitch two seed beads into centers of some rosettes.

Embellish Clock

12. Adhere fuchsia onto edge of clock face near 2:00.

13. Working clockwise, adhere rosettes at top edge of clock face, beginning near 9:00 and ending at fuchsia flower.

14. Slip teardrop beads onto each ribbon end, using embroidery needle. Knot ends one or two times past beads to secure beads in place.

15. Tie a small bow with remaining ribbon length.

16. Adhere bow onto edge of clock face at 9:00.

Tip: For a different look, spray the clock a pale blue and use tiny birds and vintage paper flowers as embellishments.

MATERIALS

(For 7" doll)

Beads: star, pink (3)

Matching thread

Porcelain and fabric baby doll, 7" tall

Ribbons:

    ¼", silk-satin, pale pink (12")

    1½", taffeta, pale pink (1¼ yds)

TOOLS

Hand-sewing needle

Tacky glue

Tape measure

An Adorable Baby Doll

For a gift or a nursery accessory, purchase a cuddly baby doll and add your own decorative touches. Ribbon loops and a set of matching "tummy" buttons transform a simple doll into something special.

MATERIALS

Beads: 11/0, seed, frosted pink

Child's white T-shirt

Embroidery floss: pale lime

Ribbon: ¼", silk-satin, pink

TOOLS

Needles:

beading

embroidery

hand-sewing

A Fancy Feminine T-shirt

HOW TO TRIM THE SHIRT

1. Thread embroidery needle with three strands of embroidery floss.

2. Hand-stitch, using a running stitch, along neck and sleeves, making ⅛"-long stitches.

3. Using beading needle, hand-stitch a seed bead between each stitch, except at center front of neck.

4. Form a rosette with pink silk-satin ribbon. Refer to Rosette on pages 12–13.

5. Using hand-sewing needle, hand-stitch rosette onto center front.

Style an ordinary T-shirt with extraordinary ribbon trim in a running stitch. Accent with beads, buttons, French knots, or ribbon roses around the neckline and sleeves.

MATERIALS FOR EACH SACHET

Flax seed (1 pound)

Lavender buds (1½ oz)

Matching thread

MATERIALS FOR YELLOW SACHET

Button: ⅜", lavender

Linens:

ivory, 8" square

yellow, 10¼" square (2)

Ribbon:

9mm, black-and-white plaid (1 yd)

Trim: black-and-white (1⅛ yds)

MATERIALS FOR LAVENDER SACHET

Fabrics:

cotton, white/ black print, 10¼" square (2)

satin, lavender, 8" square

Ribbons:

⅜", satin, lavender (1⅛ yds)

⅝", grosgrain, striped (1¼ yds)

TOOLS

Cardboard (scrap)

Fabric-marking pen

Fabric scissors

Grid-lined ruler

Hand-sewing needle

Iron and ironing board

Sewing machine

Straight pins

Tape measure

Pretty Ribbon Pillow Sachets

Delightfully scented pillow sachets are almost too pretty to hide in a drawer, but they can certainly freshen stored clothing and linens. Scent a room with lavender, roses, or herbs.

HOW TO MAKE THE YELLOW SACHET

1. Measure and mark 1" in around edges on right side of ivory linen, as shown on Yellow Sachet Diagram. Align outside edges of plaid ribbon on marks, right side up, and topstitch both edges. Press well on wrong side.

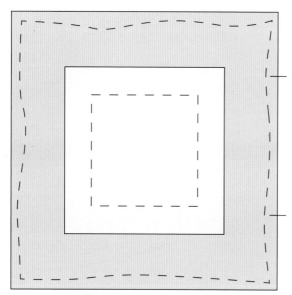

Yellow Sachet Diagram

2. Press edges of trimmed ivory linen under ½" to wrong side.

3. Center ivory square on one yellow square. Topstitch in place as shown.

4. Following diagram, mark wavy lines along outer edge of yellow linen. Trim on lines.

5. Center trimmed yellow linen on remaining yellow square, right sides facing. Using a very small stitch (1.5mm), sew together following the wavy edges. Use ½" seam allowance, and leave a 2½" opening along one side.

6. Clip bulk from corners, and seam allowance at curves up to seam line. Edge-press one layer of seam allowance open. Turn right side out through opening. Push out corners and press well.

7. Topstitch front onto back along three edges of ivory square, leaving side open that corresponds with yellow linen side-seam opening.

8. Using a funnel fashioned from cardboard scrap, fill ivory square portion of sachet with flax seeds and lavender buds.

9. Topstitch ivory square closed. Slip-stitch yellow linen outer side seam closed.

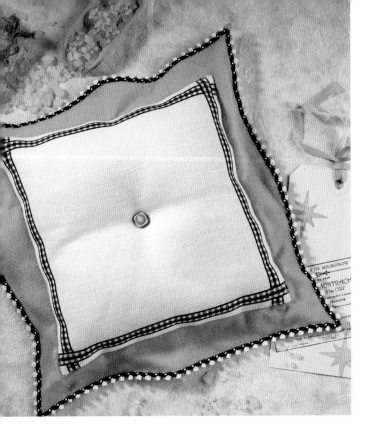

the top and bottom edges. Topstitch upper selvage edge of ribbon onto satin, leaving bow free. Press.

14. Repeat How to Make the Yellow Sachet Steps 2–3 on page 24, using a black print square and lavender satin.

15. Topstitch lavender satin ribbon onto edges of one black print square, placing ribbon 1" in from all edges. Press well.

16. Repeat How to Make the Yellow Sachet Steps 5–9 on page 24 to finish the sachet, omitting wavy edge.

10. Hand-stitch ribbon trim along outer edge.

11. Hand-stitch button onto pillow center.

HOW TO MAKE THE LAVENDER SACHET

12. Cut three 13" lengths from striped grosgrain ribbon. Fashion a 2¼"-wide tailored bow at center of each length. Wrap bow center with striped ribbon.

13. Pin three bows horizontally onto lavender satin, equal distances from each other and

MATERIALS

(For 8"-square cushion)

Button: 1", velvet-covered, black

Child's chair

Linen: white (½ yd)

Machine-embroidery thread: black

Polyester stuffing

Ribbon: 2", white/black print (2 yds)

Twill tape: ½", white (1½ yds)

TOOLS

Fabric scissors

Hand-sewing needle

Iron and ironing board

Sewing machine

Straight pins

Tape measure

Ruffled Chair Cushion

A puff of a pillow with a ruffled edge adds a charming finishing touch to diminutive furniture. Set up a small-chair vignette on a window seat, on the hearth, or in a child's playroom.

HOW TO MAKE THE CUSHION

1. For cushion top, measure chair seat. Cut two pieces from linen, using seat measurement and adding ½" all around.

2. Measure sides and front of seat, then double this measurement for ruffle length. Cut fabric 5½" wide x ruffle length. *Note: It may be necessary to seam ruffle pieces together to achieve length.*

3. Sew a narrow hem along two short edges of ruffle and press one long edge under ¾" to the wrong side. Press under ¾" again.

4. Topstitch in place along upper folded edge.

5. Position bottom edge of ribbon along hem stitching. Topstitch both ribbon edges in place.

6. Fold raw edges of ribbon to back and sew in place.

7. Machine-embroider bottom edge of ruffle, using a decorative stitch of choice.

Above: Harmonize the fabric, ruffle trim, and button with the color the chair is painted.

8. Machine-baste two rows ½" in and ⅜" in along remaining long edge for gathering. Pull gathering threads so ruffle fits three sides of cushion top.

9. Pin and sew ruffle, right sides together, onto three sides of one linen square, using a ½" seam allowance.

10. Place remaining linen square with ruffled linen square, right sides facing, making certain to pin ruffle completely out of the way of seam line.

11. Sew squares together, using a ½" seam allowance and leaving unruffled edge open. Topstitch ¼" in along first row of stitching.

A ruffled pillow can be square, round, or heart shaped. The ruffle enlarges the impact of the pillow. Buttons, ribbon roses, twists of ribbon and beaded accents make pillows more romantic and showy.

12. Clip bulk from corners. Trim seam just past outer row of stitching.

13. Turn cushion right side out and remove pins.

14. Push out corners and pull out ruffle to expose seam.

15. Press seam allowance along opened side ½" to inside.

16. Fill cushion with stuffing.

17. Cut twill tape into four equal lengths. Pin ends of two lengths into right corner and repeat for left corner of cushion opening for chair ties.

18. Topstitch opening closed catching twill tape in stitching.

19. Stitch button onto cushion center through all layers. See (1).

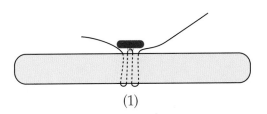

(1)

MATERIALS

Beads:

     11/0, seed, contrasting shades

     4mm, tube, pink (2)

     6mm, butterfly, yellow (6)

     6mm, flower, green (11)

     8mm, round, iridescent (6)

Button: porcelain

Fabric: broadcloth, coordinating color, 7" x 4½"

Fusible web: (3" square)

Matching thread

Phrase of choice

Ribbons:

     ⅜", grosgrain, two shades of yellow (1⅛ yds)

     size 5, wire-edged, coordinating color (10")

     scrap, yellow

TOOLS

Cardboard: 5" x 4"

Computer/word-processing program/ink-jet printer
    or photocopier

Ink-jet transfer paper

Iron and ironing board

Needles:

    beading

    large-eyed

Pencil

Press cloth

Ruler

Scissors:

    deckle-edged

    fabric

Straight pins

Tape measure

Woven

Door

Pocket

HOW TO MAKE THE DOOR POCKET

1. Using pencil and ruler, draw a 4" x 3¼" rectangle on cardboard.

2. Beginning at right-bottom corner of rectangle, pin one length of grosgrain ribbon to cardboard, with a 1¼" ribbon tail. Lay ribbon across rectangle to left-bottom corner and pin.

3. At left edge, turn grosgrain ribbon up and under at 45° angle aligning ribbon along left outside edge of rectangle. See (1). Pin fold to cardboard. Turn ribbon down at 45° angle. Pin fold to cardboard and lay ribbon across rectangle to right edge, aligning ribbon.

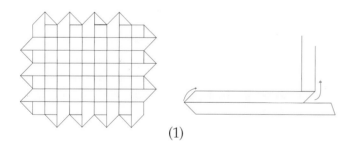

(1)

4. Repeat folding and pinning at right edge as in Step 3, bringing ribbon across to left edge. Continue in this manner, ending with 1¼" tail at top-left corner.

5. Thread large-eyed needle with second length of grosgrain ribbon. Working vertically from bottom-

left corner, weave ribbon through first the length, following Steps 2–4. End with a 1¼" tail at the top-right corner.

6. Remove pins from cardboard. Tuck and press tails under woven piece.

7. Iron fusible web to underside of woven ribbon, following manufacturer's instructions.

8. Press broadcloth under ½" to wrong side along each 4½" edge. Fold fabric in half, right sides together, lining up short edges. See (2).

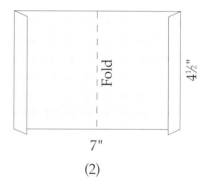

(2)

9. Sew the sides, with ¼" seam allowance, leaving folded edge open at pocket top. See (3). Turn right side out and press. Fuse to woven ribbon.

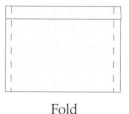

Fold

(3)

10. Have phrase copied onto transfer paper or, using computer, create a phrase and print backward onto transfer paper.

11. Transfer printed phrase onto woven ribbon, following manufacturer's instructions.

12. Double thread length in beading needle and adjust so looped end is longer. Beginning at left-bottom corner, pass needle through fabric or ribbon. Before pulling thread through, slip needle through loop and pull taut, locking thread in place.

13. Slip specialty beads onto thread, alternating with seed beads. Plan for a seed bead as first and last beads. Stitch around last seed bead then back up through beads of each dangle. Stitch back into ribbon and whipstitch to secure. Vary bead combinations.

14. Invisibly run thread to next bead placement. Take two whipstitches to secure thread, then slip on specialty beads.

15. Using large-eyed needle, anchor 16" length of quadrupled thread to pocket top at one side. Alternate 10 seed beads and specialty beads to form 7" hanger.

16. Secure thread end to pocket top at other side.

Make Pansy Embellishment

17. Mark wire-edged ribbon at 3" and 4" intervals. See (1).

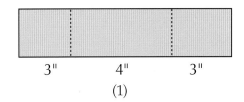

3"   4"   3"

(1)

18. Fold ends under. Gather-stitch along dashed line. See (2).

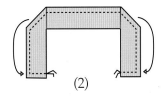

(2)

19. Gather and secure thread to form petals. Join last petal to first. Completed Pansy. See (3).

(3)

20. Stitch a specialty bead onto pansy center. Stitch pansy onto top of beaded hanger.

21. Stitch button onto pocket front with narrow ribbon.

MATERIALS FOR EACH ORNAMENT

Glass oval: 3" x 5" with drilled hole

Ribbon: ⅜", silk-satin, aqua (⅔ yd)

FOR BUTTON ORNAMENT:

Buttons: assorted sizes, mother-of-pearl (approx. 50)

Pearls: 6mm, blush (3)

FOR VINTAGE JEWELRY ORNAMENT:

Bracelet: 6"

Jewelry: small pieces (10)

FOR ROSETTE ORNAMENT:

Ribbons: 4mm, silk, 5", assorted colors (20)

TOOLS

E-6000 adhesive   Tape measure

Toothpick

Sparkling Glass Ornaments

HOW TO MAKE THE ORNAMENTS

Button Ornament

1. Arrange 2–3 layers of buttons around outer edge. Using toothpick, adhere in place. Adhere pearls in place where desired.

Vintage Jewelry Ornament

2. Arrange bracelet and jewelry pieces around outer edge. Using toothpick, adhere in place.

Rosette Ornament

3. Make 19 rosettes. Refer to Make Rosette on pages 12–13. Using toothpick, adhere the rosettes in place.

Grouped or singly, glass disk ornaments can twinkle for beauty and safety in your windows. No more collisions for birds or children who mistake windows for "air" when these beribboned beauties call attention to themselves.

MATERIALS

Beads:

    11/0, seed, five colors

    4mm, pearls, ecru (7)

Fabric scraps:

    satin or silk,

        lavender, mauve, silver (7)

        green, (3)

Interfacing: lightweight, nonwoven, 8" square

Matching thread

Polyester stuffing

Silk dupioni: moss green (¼ yd)

Silk ribbon: 4mm, heather (1¼ yds)

Straight pins

Velvet: moss green (¼ yd)

TOOLS

Fabric-marking pen: fine tip, brown

Fabric scissors

Iron and ironing board

Metal ruler

Needles:

    embroidery

    hand-sewing

Permanent ink pen

Sewing machine

Tape measure

Crazy-quilted Pillow

Ribbons and beads really shine on a unique pillow with a crazy-quilt-block design. The special touches come in adding ribbon and bead accents on quilting seams and around pillow edge.

Make Quilt Block

1. Enlarge 134% and photocopy Cabbage Rose Pattern. Transfer patterns of one unit each for A, B, and C onto a foundation of non-woven interfacing or batiste fabric, using a ruler, permanent ink pen, and a light source. Add ¼" seam allowance to all edges.

2. Using lavender, silver, and mauve fabrics for rose petals, moss green dupioni for background, and green scraps for leaves, foundation-piece the units.

3. Cut rectangular fabric pieces for each numbered section 1" larger all around. Cut generic sizes in order to piece multiple sections.

4. With foundation unmarked side up, place fabric piece for section 1 over section 1, right side up. Pin in place. Pin fabric piece for section 2 onto fabric piece 1, right sides facing.

5. Turn foundation over, with marked side up. Sew along line between sections 1 and 2, using a very small stitch, beginning and ending 2–3 stitches beyond line.

6. Trim excess fabric ⅛" past seam line. Turn over. Open fabric piece 2 and finger-press seam.

7. Pin fabric piece for section 3 onto fabric piece 2, right sides facing. Proceed as in Steps 5–6. Continue in this manner to foundation-piece each unit.

8. For those spaces with a double mark, stitch two fabric pieces together before stitching the fabric in place.

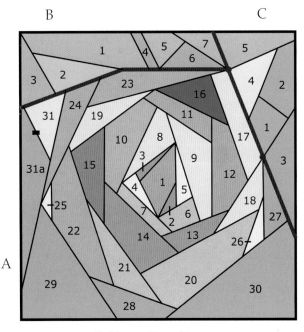

Cabbage Rose Pattern

Enlarge 134%

9. Trim all seam allowances on each unit. Sew the units together in alphabetical order. Press seam allowances open.

Make Pillow

10. Cut two 4½" x 1¼" strips and two 6" x 1¼" strips from moss green velvet. Sew the 4½" strips onto block sides. Press seam allowance toward strips. Sew 6" strips onto top and bottom of block, pressing seam allowance toward strips.

11. Cut a 6" square from the velvet. Pin and sew velvet square onto the bordered block, right sides facing, using ¼" seam allowance and leaving 3" opening along one side.

12. Clip bulk from corners and turn pillow right side out. Fill firmly with polyester stuffing. Hand-stitch opening closed.

Cascade Stitch

13. Stitch or glue bow knot onto fabric. Thread embroidery needle with ribbon length. Allow ribbon to twist. Go down at A. See (1).

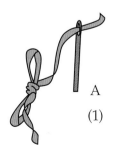

(1)

14. Come up at B and go down at C, making a small backstitch to hold cascade in place. Come up at D. See (2). Repeat for desired length. Cascade-stitch around seamed edges of pillow. Stitch pearls onto cascading stitches in a pleasing arrangement.

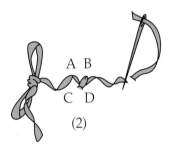

A B
C D
(2)

Embellish Pillow

15. Using straight pins to hold beads in place, accent pillow with seed beads along seam lines of design.

Tip: This small pillow can be filled with lavender or other potpourri. Whenever putting flowers or herbs inside of a handmade piece, make a small inner pillow that can be filled with the sachet to keep the oils from seeping onto the outer fabric. When inserting the inner sachet pillow, tack to the inside corners of the outer pillow so the sachet stays evenly distributed.

MATERIALS

Acrylic paints:

    green

    off-white

    pearlescent

Silk ribbons:

    7mm, (18" each)

        apricot

        bright pink

        light orange

        orchid

        rich rose

    13mm, leaf green (1¼ yds)

Stretched canvas: 5" x 7"

TOOLS

Darning needle

Foam paintbrush

Iron and ironing board

Large paper bag

Paint palette

Pencils: (2)

Tacky glue

Tape measure

Stripes of Ribbons & Bows

Easy to do and pretty to display, this mini canvas gets a smart stripe treatment in paint and ribbons. Hang it on a doorknob, a wall, or tassel style from a peg on an outer closet door. Use the suggested colors here or select colors that match your home decor.

HOW TO MAKE THE DISPLAY

1. Cover the work surface with paper bag.

2. Use off-white paint mixed with green paint to create two shades of pastel green paint.

3. Paint the canvas with an uneven narrow-striped pattern.

4. When dry, brush over stripe pattern with watered-down coat of pearlescent paint. Let dry.

Make Pencil Violet

5. Press 18" lengths of the 7mm silk ribbon.

6. Using pencils held closely together, slip one 7mm ribbon length between pencils so the center of ribbon length is near the middle of the pencils.

7. Weave ribbon around pencils so that each pencil has 2–3 loops of ribbon. See (1).

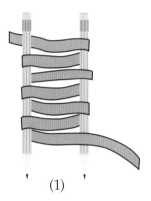

(1)

8. Take top end of ribbon and wrap it down toward back, under, and up around center two times, cinching ribbon loops together. See (2).

(2)

Tip: When creating the ribbon bands, try leaving them unattached in the middle so that small items such as school pictures or other little keepsakes can be placed under the ribbons and displayed as a miniature bulletin board.

42

9. Take opposite end of ribbon and wrap it up toward front, under, and up around center, cinching ribbon loops tighter. Make certain ribbon ends are opposite each other once center has been cinched. See (3).

(3)

10. Tie ribbon ends in a double knot at center of one side. Slip violet off pencils. See (4).

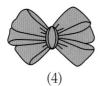

(4)

Embellish Canvas

11. Arrange ribbon shades about 1" apart and glue violets onto canvas.

When deciding where to hang your new mini canvas, try making several in coordinating colors and different sizes to hang in a grouping on your wall. Several of the same item can make a dramatic statement.

12. Extend ribbon ends around to back side of canvas and glue ends in place.

13. Cut a 7" length from 13mm silk ribbon. Press both ribbon lengths.

14. Glue short length onto top and upper sides of canvas.

15. Make a pencil violet near center of 13mm ribbon, extending the width of petals.

16. With bow extended about 1½" above canvas, glue remainder of ribbon length onto sides and bottom of canvas.

MATERIALS

Elastic: ¼" (¼ yd)

Matching thread

Ribbon: ⅝", red brocade (½ yd)

Watch face with pins

TOOLS

Fabric scissors   Sewing machine

Hand-sewing needle   Tape measure

HOW TO MAKE THE WATCHBAND

1. Measure the circumference of the wrist and cut the elastic to this measurement plus ½".

2. Cut 1½" piece from red brocade ribbon. Cut remaining length in half.

3. Slip one length through both watchband pins and center.

4. Place second ribbon length along first, wrong sides facing. Whipstitch long edges together, leaving ends open.

5. Slip elastic between ribbon lengths. Be certain to secure elastic at one end before exiting and securing opposite end.

6. Sew all ribbon and elastic ends together, with top sides facing, using ¼" seam allowance.

7. Wrap seam with 1½" ribbon and invisibly hand-stitch in place.

Whimsical Watchband

Watches make a personal style statement, and this example is no exception. Purchase one, or a few, inexpensive wrist watches to enhance and coordinate with a ribbon wristband for each of your favorite outfits.

MATERIALS

Beads: assortment including seed beads

Matching thread

Purchased mesh luminaria: 2½" x 4" tall, bag
    shaped (1)

Ribbon: 20mm, velvet, frill-edged, black (⅝ yd)

TOOLS

Beading needle

Hot-glue gun and glue sticks

Large paper bag

Tape measure

Beaded Mesh Luminaria

Center one on each of your tables for a safe and lovely candlelit dining experience, or perhaps one at each place setting. They can become guest take-home gifts for a party.

HOW TO EMBELLISH LUMINARIA

1. Cover work surface with paper bag. Measure circumference of luminaria base and cut velvet ribbon to this measurement.

2. Cut a second length of velvet ribbon and form a tailored bow. Center and glue bow onto first ribbon length. Cut a third length from velvet ribbon and wrap around center of bow, gluing ends onto back of first length.

3. Wrap embellished ribbon around luminaria base and glue in place.

4. Thread needle with doubled strand. Align ends and knot, so thread is quadrupled.

5. Stitch thread into top corner of luminaria. Whipstitch again in same location.

6. Slip beads onto thread in a pleasing arrangement to create bead drape, using seed beads between larger beads.

7. When satisfied with length of bead drape, stitch thread into next top corner of luminaria, securing thread.

8. Continue to slip beads onto thread to create bead drapes. Anchor drapes at corners.

Tip: Fine-grain sand, glass marbles, glass beads, coffee grounds, stones, or fish-tank gravel are all acceptable "beds" for the support of the candle and to prevent stains and burns from dripping hot wax as the candle burns down.

It is easy to make or remake small beaded accent pieces. Individual beads can be strung on thin wire and then bent into shapes like hearts or stars. Beaded pieces from a broken broach or necklace can be added to other treasures such as vintage bottles or boxes.

Simple beading is an accent that makes the ordinary extraordinary. This small purchased lamp shade had its beaded exterior further embellished by the addition of small droplet style beads.

49

MATERIALS

(For 9"-square box)

Acrylic paint: light tan

Buttons: 1" or larger, mother-of-pearl (4)

Card: new or vintage

Leaves:

    natural skeleton (2)

    satin, ecru (2)

Papier-mâché box: 9" square

Ribbon scraps

Rose petals: dried

Rosebuds: small, lavender (6)

Sequins: 15mm, iridescent (2)

Tissue papers: printed, three assorted
    (1–2 sheets each)

Vintage lace scraps

TOOLS

Decoupage medium

E6000 adhesive

Foam paintbrush

Large paper bag

Sea sponge

Button & Lace Gift Box

Though this gift may well be for yourself, a beautiful box is a treasure even before the box is filled. A purchased box can be enhanced with decoupaged lace, ribbons, beads, bits and trims, and finished off with buttons as a border on the sides.

HOW TO MAKE THE GIFT BOX

1. Cover work surface with large paper bag.

2. Tear tissues into pieces and crumple, then smooth out.

3. Randomly decoupage tissue pieces onto surfaces of box, inside and out. Overlap all pieces. Let dry.

4. Lightly sponge paint onto decoupaged box.

5. Decoupage pieces of ribbon, lace, card, and individual rose petals onto lid.

6. Decoupage a piece of bias-cut ribbon onto lid sides.

7. Glue rosebuds onto edge of lid as shown in photo on page 51.

8. Coat all surfaces of the box with a second application of decoupage medium. Let dry.

9. Glue the buttons onto the lid and sides as desired.

10. Glue the sequins onto the lid as desired.

Tip: Handmade boxes can be embellished in an endless number of ways. In place of paper, adhere fabric and add "rescued" pieces from old quilts and vintage jewelry to adorn both the lid and the sides. Make the boxes large enough to store keepsakes from the years your son was growing up, your daughter's wedding day, or a memorable trip taken with a girlfriend.

Smaller boxes can hold secrets such as a ticket stub from your first date or the pin you were given during your sorority days in college.

Beaded-fruit Wreath

MATERIALS

Beaded pears: small (12)

Glittered bead sprays: large, wired, pale gold (3)

Ribbons:

    1", sheer, pale yellow (1¼ yds)

    1½", double-faced satin, ivory (1 yd)

Wire: 18-gauge, silver (27")

TOOLS

Fabric scissors

Knitting needle

Needle-nosed pliers

Tape measure

Wire cutters

A dewy delicious appeal can be given to tiny fruit shapes with transparent beads. Arrange and attach an array of beaded fruits or vegetables onto a wreath framework. Display the finished wreath in the dining room, the kitchen, or atop a gift box.

HOW TO MAKE THE WREATH

1. Using needle-nosed pliers, bend a loop at one end of wire length.

2. Push opposite wire end through each beaded pear, positioning pear slightly offset from vertical center.

Tip: You may find it helpful to first pierce a hole into the pear, using a knitting needle or other tool. Wiring step will be easier to do.

3. Slip pears onto wire so that stem on each is upright. To accomplish this, slip six pears onto wire, stem side down, and remaining six pears onto wire, stem side up.

4. Form wire into circular shape and slip straight wire end through looped wire end. Adjust until look is "full."

5. Trim excess wire from straight end, leaving a ½". Bend straight end around looped end to secure.

6. Separate large bead sprays into clusters of three to four beads.

7. Wrap a cluster between each pear.

8. Beginning between top center pears, wrap yellow ribbon several times around wire to cover it.

9. Extend the ribbon to the next space between pears, finishing at top center.

10. Tie ribbon ends together in a knot and trim off excess ribbon.

11. Slip the center of ivory ribbon between top center pears.

12. Tie ribbon in a soft knot onto wire. Extend ribbon ends upward about 5" and tie in a soft bow. Pull loops to tighten. Using a "fork cut", trim ribbon ends.

Tip: To make this easy wreath a keepsake, use a strand of beads from a childhood necklace, strung on wire, in place of bead sprays to wrap around the fruit on the wreath.

Simple wreaths can be made from an endless number of objects. The wreath below was made by wrapping a metal ring with velvet ribbon and then attaching velvet flowers and fabric buds. Even a small paper "fan" pin was added to the assortment.

Beaded fruit need not always be store bought. These beaded strawberries were made by rolling small plastic strawberries in seed and bugle beads. For a touch of realism, small velvet leaves were glued to the finished berries. They are easily made and beautiful to arrange in a bowl or on a wreath.

MATERIALS

Beads:

    11/0, seed beads, 12 assorted floral shades in amber, copper, brown, burgundy, plum

    six assorted leaf-green shades

    4mm, round or diamond crystal, black or smoke (11)

Ribbons:

    7mm, silk, hunter green (1 yd)

    52mm, taffeta picot, terra-cotta (⅝ yd)

Velvet leaves:

        green variegated (5)

        purple variegated (5)

Wire: 26-gauge, metallic plum (8½ yds)

TOOLS

Needle-nosed pliers

Tacky glue

Tape measure

Wire cutters

Beaded Rose

An elegant long-stemmed rose can be long lasting with this beaded beauty. As a gift or decorative display item, it will be remembered for its exquisite personally crafted detail. The glistening effect of translucent beads lends the rose a dew-kissed appearance.

Form Petal

1. Cut wire into eleven 30" lengths. Tie a knot at one end of each length of wire.

2. Position five amber seed beads onto wire 2" below knot.

3. Extend wire 3" below bottom bead and fold back up.

4. Tightly wrap wire around itself just below bottom bead. Wire will extend to left of center axis.

5. Pull wire taut using needle-nosed pliers. See (1).

(1)

6. Beginning at base of axis, slightly bend wire.

7. Slide eight beads onto wire and bend beaded wire to lie tightly next to left side of axis.

8. Tightly wind wire around first bead on axis, taking wire to back side of axis first. Wire will extend to right of axis. See (2).

(2)

9. Continue beading each row, adding beads to accommodate length of row to end of axis. Repeat shaping process for each row. For center petal, there will be five rows of beads on each side of center axis.

10. Make certain to straighten axis after each row of beads has been added. See (3).

(3)

11. Work petal from facing side with each row and wrap wire around axis from back to front. *Note: Wire wrappings on one side will be more obvious—this will be back side.*

12. Repeat Steps 5–7. Petal size is dependent on number of beaded rows wired to basic axis.

13. There will be three wires now at base of petal, one that is looped. Trim loop 1" below petal base and extend wire. This will be used to wire petals together.

14. Tightly twist remaining wires around petal base and trim excess. Be careful to not over-twist.

15. Flatten extending wire against twists, using pliers.

16. Cut knot from top of axis wire, then fold down to back of petal.

17. Tightly wrap wire around bottom of axis twice. Cut looped wire near base of axis and straighten wire. Twist wires and trim.

18. Form beaded shapes into leaves or petals by bending wires as desired as each row is beaded.

Make Rose

19. Make 10 more petals, layering rows around center petal, with each graduating in color from light to dark.

20. Slip 2–3 4mm diamond or round crystal beads onto wire when forming last row on four petals.

Form Leaf

21. Working with 20" wire length, make one small leaf using green seed beads, forming three rows around center axis.

22. Cut three 25" lengths from wire. Make three large leaves, using green seed beads and forming five rows around axis.

23. Twist leaves together and cover wire with silk ribbon, as if using florist tape. Glue as needed.

24. Glue one green and one purple velvet leaves together, wrong sides facing. Repeat with remaining velvet leaves.

25. Arrange velvet leaves around the rose. Cover the wire with silk ribbon as above.

26. Tie taffeta ribbon around stem and into a small bow.

Tip: Small beaded flowers can have their stems wrapped in ribbon to be used as a corsage or boutonniere for a special wedding.

MATERIALS

Assorted trims: 3"–6" scraps (35–40)

  braids

  laces

  ribbons

Papers: assorted pastels

Poster board

Ribbon: ¼", satin, coordinating color (3½ yds)

TOOLS

Glue stick

Large paper bag

Pencils (2)

Scissors:

  craft

  scallop-edged

Tacky glue

Tape measure

Teardrop-shaped paper punch

A Treasure of Trimmed Tags

Personally embellished gift tags will be the most unique and memorable of any the lucky recipient receives. For any season or holiday, trim scraps enhance store-bought gift tags. Edge and stripe them to your heart's content..

HOW TO MAKE THE TAGS

1. Cover the work surface with large paper bag.

2. Using craft scissors, cut two tags for every finished tag from the poster board, using Tag Pattern below. Trim the bottom edges, using scallop-edged scissors.

3. Using tacky glue, adhere the pastel paper onto one of the tags. Using craft scissors, trim the paper to expose the tag's scalloped edge.

4. Trim paper flush to tag sides and triangular top.

5. Punch hole at top of each tag.

6. Arrange trims as desired on the paper-covered tag. Tightly wrap trim scraps around tag, using glue stick to hold trims in place on back side. Adhere the untrimmed tag onto back of the embellished tag with tacky glue.

7. Cut ribbon into 18" lengths.

8. Slip satin ribbon through teardrop hole. Tie ribbon ends into a bow for a hanger.

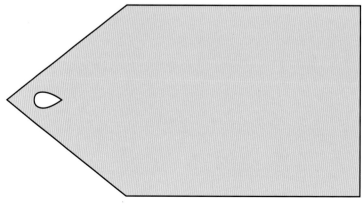

Tag Pattern

64

Small tags can be used to make any occasion a bit more special. When making tags, use scraps from worn baby dresses or your children's hair ribbons that you could not bear to throw away.

Tags can also be made to match the gift that is being given. When making a scrapbook for a friend to record memories of her baby, make the tags with the same materials used for binding the outside of the scrapbook.

Tip: When making tags, do not wrap the pieces around to the back. Cut them the same size as the tag and attach them only to the front so a message can be written on the reverse side of the tag.

MATERIALS

Decorative papers: 12" square (1–2 each)

    lavender floral

    lavender tone-on-tone

    sage tone-on-tone

Ribbon garland: ⅜", silk, lavender/orchid (2 yds)

Ribbons:

    ¼", embellished satin, pale sage (1½ yds)

    ⅜", grosgrain, taupe olive (2 yds)

    20mm, frill organdy, light grass green (¾ yd)

Sheet of small-sized printed paper frames

Small letter holder

TOOLS

Clear no-gloss varnish

Foam brush

Large paper bag

Scissors:

    craft

    deckle-edged

    fabric

Tacky glue

Tape measure

Floral Letter Holder

Collect your bills and personal mail, in and out-going, in a stylish letter holder. Select printed paper in a colored pattern, and pretty ribbon to accent the eventual hanging place for your letter holder. No more misplaced correspondence—and how charming!

HOW TO MAKE LETTER HOLDER

1. Using craft scissors, cut the lavender floral and sage tone-on-tone papers to size so that all front surfaces of the letter holder can be re-covered with new paper.

2. Brush tacky glue, watered down to a paint-like consistency, onto back of paper and cover letter holder.

3. Glue the grosgrain ribbon onto the front pocket edges with tacky glue.

4. Glue ribbon garland trim onto top of grosgrain ribbon.

5. Glue the ribbon garland onto the top edges.

6. Cover the bottom and side edges with satin ribbon and glue in place.

7. Using deckle-edged scissors, trim around three of the paper frames.

8. Cut a piece from lavender tone-on-tone paper to fit within each frame.

9. Using glue stick, glue a frame onto front of each pocket.

10. Coat entire letter holder with varnish. Let dry.

11. Cut a 6"–7" length from frilly organdy ribbon. Trim ends with a "fork cut."

12. Tie a knot at center of length and glue knot onto center of framed pieces. Glue ends in place as well.

Letter holders such as this one are easy enough to make for every room in the house. Use them in the bath to hold those special items reserved for quiet moments or in a teenage daughter's room to hold her dance pictures and private notes.

Tip: Photocopy these labels or create your own to add a personalized flair to each letter holder.

Hair and Nails

Bath

Lotion

69

MATERIALS

Covered wire: 28-gauge, green

Ribbons:

    1½", hand-dyed bias cut,

        celery green (1½ yds)

        coral rose (1½ yds = one full rose)

        cream with lavender edges
        (1½ yds = one full rose)

        cream with pale pink edges
        (3 yds = one full rose and three rosebuds)

        mint green (1 yd)

        pale lavender (1 yd = two rosebuds)

        pinky mauve (3 yds = six rosebuds)

    75mm, pleat georgette, pale pink (1 yd)

Matching threads

TOOLS

Fabric scissors

Hand-sewing needle

Needle-nosed pliers

Tacky glue

Tape measure

Wire cutters

Ribbon Rose Bouquet

This lush rose bouquet is created more easily than it appears. Ribbon rose blossoms in delicate colors will last as a keepsake for years. Whether one bouquet as a graceful gift or a matched array in a series of vases on the mantel, the effect will be memorable.

1. Cut 1½" ribbons to make rose-buds and roses. For each rose-bud, cut an 18" length. For each full rose, cut a 54" length.

2. Cut one 8" length from wire for each rosebud and rose. Using needle-nosed pliers, fold one end of wire down ¼", forming a small loop.

Make Rosebud

3. Fold ribbon down at right angle. See (1). Place looped end of wire in the center of fold so wire is not visible above fold. Whipstitch wire to ribbon through loop.

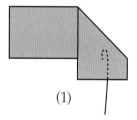

(1)

4. Fold ribbon again. See (2). Roll ribbon and wire between fingers in direction of fold to end of right-angle fold.

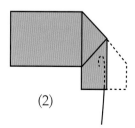

(2)

5. Gather-stitch remaining length of the ribbon. Taper stitches at ribbon end. See (3).

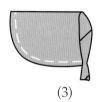

(3)

6. Pull gathers slightly. Loosely cup gathered ribbon around center ribbon roll.

7. Gather tightly and secure thread. Completed Rosebud. See (4).

(4)

Attach Leaf

8. Cut a 3" length from celery or mint green ribbon for each rosebud leaf.

9. Fold ribbon in half, matching short ends.

10. Place cut ends of folded leaf against rosebud and stitch onto rosebud base.

Make Full Rose

11. After completing Steps 3–4 on page 72, continue by gathering the entire length of ribbon, working with manageable lengths, and loosely cupping ribbon around center. Taper stitches at ribbon end.

12. Cut five 9" lengths from celery or mint green ribbon.

13. Cut ribbon lengths into three ½"-wide strips. Glue end of one cut strip onto a rose base.

14. Wrap wire with ribbon, as if using florist tape. Repeat with each rose and rosebud.

Assemble Bouquet

15. Arrange roses and rosebuds, then wire together near bases.

16. Gather-stitch one long edge of georgette ribbon and form ribbon into a ruffled cuff.

17. Secure stitches and slip cuff up underneath roses.

18. Secure cuff in place with a length of celery green ribbon tied in a bow.

Such beautifully designed and ever-lasting bouquets can be used as a bridesmaid bouquet. Make it from the same ribbons that adorn the dresses worn on this special day.

MATERIALS

Cord: ⅛", light blue (1 yd)

Silk dupioni:

    lavender (¼ yd)

    olive green (⅜ yd)

Slubbed satin: light blue, 9" x 20"

Grommets: dark green (10)

Interfacing: heavy-weight (7" circle)

Matching thread

Ribbon: 50mm, satin polka dot, deep fuchsia
    (1⅛ yds)

TOOLS

Fabric-marking pen: fine tip

Fabric scissors

Grommet tool

Iron and ironing board

Sewing machine

Straight pins

Tape measure

Ribbon - banded Drawstring Bag

For a quick overnight bag or a guest room gift, particularly when the bath is down the hall, prepare a glamourous drawstring bag. Choose lovely fabrics for outside and lining and accent with contrasting wide ribbons.

HOW TO MAKE BAG

1. From lavender silk, cut a 4" x 20" piece and a 7" circle. From olive silk, cut a 13" x 20" piece and a 7" circle.

2. Sew 4" x 20" silk onto 9" x 20" satin right sides facing, aligning 20" edges and using ½" seam allowance. Press seam allowance open.

3. Sew the 13" x 20" silk onto remaining long edge of the lavender silk. Press seam allowances open.

4. Mark 1⅞" down along lavender and blue fabric seam line.

5. Cut fuchsia ribbon in half. Align one selvage edge of ribbon, right sides up, along marks and sew in place.

6. Trim ribbon ends flush with fabric edges.

7. Align one selvage edge of remaining ribbon along lavender and blue fabric seam line at top of first ribbon. Sew in place and press.

When making bags such as this one it can be a wonderful gift idea for someone in the hospital to line the inside of the bag with a thin waterproof liner and then use it to cover the vase of flowers that can be hand delivered. When the flowers have long since been discarded the bag can be used to store anything from a necessity to something frivolous.

8. Fold piece in half, right sides facing, so ribbon ends are aligned.

9. Pin in place and sew, using a ½" seam allowance. Press seam allowance open.

10. Fold olive silk down, wrong sides facing, to inside of tube, leaving a ½" olive border showing above lavender. Press to form top edge of bag.

11. On work surface, layer and pin lavender circle wrong side up, interfacing, and olive circle right side up.

Tips: This little bag is ideal for holding toothpaste and brush, cosmetics, a lace teddy, body wash, and other personal items. An alternative for the beach is to use hardy fabrics and a waterproof lining material to hold a wet bikini.

For an unusual twist try it as a vase for a lovely floral arrangement.

12. Pin layered bottom onto raw edges of tube with lavender and blue right sides facing.

13. Sew, using ½" seam allowance. Sew again ⅛" in along first row. Trim seam close to outside seam.

14. Overcast seam. Turn bag right side out.

15. Center and mark the placement for the grommets 1⅞" apart around lavender strip.

16. Using tool, insert grommets through both fabric layers. Slip cord in and out of grommets for bag closure.

MATERIALS

Beads:

    8/0 seed, hex cut, platinum

    4mm, faceted round, amber (approx. 23)

    6mm, round, amber (8)

    6mm, specialty, amber (1)

    8mm, oval specialty (1)

    standard-sized bugle, gold (11)

Brocade: metallic gold (1 yd)

Embroidery floss: metallic gold

Journal: 6" x 9"

Matching thread

Ribbons:

    ⅝", silk-satin, pale gold (¼ yd)

    1¾", velvet, plum (⅜ yd)

Taffeta: cross-dyed, gold (⅜ yd)

Vintage lace: 12" (1 yd)

Wire: 24-gauge, gold (18")

TOOLS

Bias turner

Iron and ironing board

Fabric scissors

Needle-nosed pliers

Needles:

    darning

    embroidery

Sewing machine

Straight pins

Tape measure

Wire cutters

Embellished Journal Jacket

A fabric book or journal jacket makes a lovely gift for a loved one, especially when embellished with lace, velvet, metallic thread, and a beaded initial for the cover or as a bookmark.

HOW TO COVER THE JOURNAL

1. From taffeta, cut one 6" x 10" front piece; two 6¼" x 10" pocket pieces; one 13" x 10" lining piece. Cut one 1" x 3" piece along bias of taffeta. From brocade, cut one 8" x 10" spine/back piece.

2. Sew spine/back piece onto front, right sides facing, aligning 10" edges and using a ½" seam allowance. Press seam allowance open.

3. On the right side of the fabric, sew lace and velvet ribbon over the seam.

4. Fold bias piece in half, right sides facing. Sew ⅛" in from folded edge.

5. Turn right side out. With cover right side up, loop bias piece and baste-stitch ends onto center of right-hand edge.

6. Baste-stitch end of silk ribbon onto left-center edge.

7. Sew a narrow hem along one 10" edge of each pocket.

8. Topstitch edge of lace over hemmed edge.

9. Pin opposite edges of pockets to left and right edge of outer cover, right sides facing.

Genteel ladies appreciated the finer enhancements of favored objects. Among these were books and private journals bound in embossed leather. An interpretation for today combined with pleasing visual sparkle in a meaningful initial tribute. The lace spine of the book jacket matches the inside lace-edged pockets that hold the cover, front and back. The soft touch of velvet for thumb and fingers embraces the book for reading or writing. Books of old were monogrammed with embossing. In that spirit, our lady's version incorporates her beaded-wire "illuminated" capital for bookmark or ornament.

10. Pin and sew lining over outer cover/pockets, right sides facing. Use ⅜" seam allowance and leave 3" opening along back bottom edge.

11. Clip corners and turn right side out through opening.

12. Press and slip-stitch opening closed, using darning needle.

13. Slip journal into jacket pockets. Using Cascade Stitch, embroider along seam around edge of cover, using metallic embroidery floss. Refer to Cascade Stitch on page 39.

Make Beaded Initial

14. Wrap one wire end three times around needle-nosed pliers, forming tight coils.

15. Arrange and slip beads onto wire. Form letter of choice with wire as if writing a letter script style.

16. Anchor wire to itself as necessary and coil end.

17. Tie beaded initial onto the velvet ribbon with a length of metallic floss.

Tip: When making a beaded alphabet it is sometimes easier to buy small metal or wooden letters and use those as the "form" to shape the beaded wire around.

MATERIALS

Assorted decorative fibers: five or more types and colors (3 yds ea)

Flower petals: silk hydrangea

Machine-embroidery threads:

    light olive

    olive

    additional pastel shades (4)

Pillow form: satin, lavender (12" square)

Ribbons:

    ⅜", satin, olive (3 yds)

    1½", satin, blue (2 yds)

    4mm–5mm, seven or more assorted types and colors (3 yds ea)

Vintage lace scraps

Water-soluble adhesive sheet (22" square)

Water-soluble film sheet (22" square)

TOOLS

Bath towel

Cutting mat

Grid-lined ruler

Rotary cutter

Sewing machine

Tape measure

Ribbon-lace Pillow

The fragile appearance of this beautiful pillow is deceiving. Appearing composed of colorful cobwebs and air, its ribbons and threads are firmly stitched in a mesh effect. A bright pillow inside and a ribbon tie style this delicate "look."

HOW TO MAKE THE LACE
Make Ribbon Lace

1. Place the adhesive sheet on work surface, adhesive side up. *Note: It may be necessary to piece sheet.*

2. Place fibers diagonally in both directions from corner to corner, working 2–3 pieces into the corners. Press assortment of fibers and ribbons onto adhesive in continuous 3-yd strips. *Note: The spaces between the various fibers, trims, and ribbons can be from ½"–1½" apart.*

3. Lay fibers vertically and horizontally in slightly haphazard fashion from corner to corner, until entire piece of adhesive has been crisscrossed with fibers and ribbon. See (1).

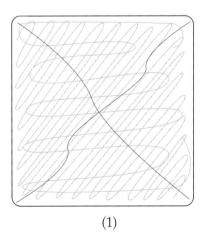

(1)

4. Randomly place bits of torn lace scraps and individual flower petals onto adhesive.

5. Place film sheet on top of covered adhesive sheet.

6. Sew with olive embroidery thread, through all layers and throughout entire piece in a vertical and horizontal grid maintaining ¾" space between the grid-sewn lines.

7. Meander-stitch entire piece with remaining embroidery threads. See (2).

(2)

8. Using grid-lined ruler and rotary cutter, trim ribbon lace to 20" square.

9. Place the satin ribbon, right sides facing, along one edge of lace. Beginning at one corner, sew along the inner-selvage edge of ribbon around the outside edge of the lace, overlapping ends ¼". Miter-fold the ribbon at each corner.

10. Sew a second seam around the ribbon ¹⁄₁₆" in from the first seam.

11. Fill the kitchen sink with warm water.

12. Fold the lace to lie flat in sink. Place lace in water and gently swish it around until the water-soluble products have completely dissolved.

13. Carefully rinse lace in slightly soapy warm water. Rinse again in clear water.

14. Place lace flat on towel. Roll up the towel to absorb the excess water.

15. Place lace on flat surface to dry. Carefully press.

16. Wrap ribbon lace around pillow form. See (3).

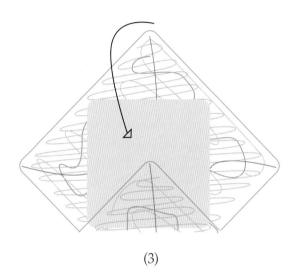

(3)

17. Tie 1½" satin ribbon into a bow around pillow to secure.

Tip: Using this lace technique, pieces of fabric can be made large enough to actually design wearable art such as vests or bags.

MATERIALS

Matching thread

Ribbon: 1½", jacquard (2 yds)

Shell-fringe tape: 2" (¾ yd)

Straw handbag

Vintage lace: ½" (1 yd)

TOOLS

Fabric scissors

Hand-sewing needle

Iron and ironing board

Sewing machine

Tacky glue

Tape measure

Bead & Seashell Bag

A purchased handbag becomes a fabulous fashion accessory with the addition of lace, ribbons, and bead and seashell trim. Stitch on these simple embellishments for an outing to a beach or a cruise.

Cut handle from bag.

Measure around top edge of handbag. Cut shell-fringe tape to this measurement. Cut ribbon and lace to this measurement plus 1".

Hand-stitch edge of shell-fringe tape onto handbag, 1¼" down from top edge.

Sew top edge of lace under one long edge of ribbon, right sides up. Press.

Tips: Once your handbag is styled with ribbon and bead/shell trim, you can have fun creating complementary items. For the beach or a patio party, a matching colored straw sun hat can be made. Stitch on a ribbon and bead/shell trim for a stylish hatband.

To bring the outfit "look" together, ribbons, shells, and beads can be added to a swimsuit cover-up, jacket, or wrap, and even to the edge of a sun umbrella.

Fold ribbon and lace in half, matching all the ends. Sew ends together, using a ½" seam allowance. Press the seam allowance open and set aside.

Working with remaining ribbon length, press both selvages under to wrong side about ⁵⁄₁₆" along entire length of ribbon.

Glue edges in place, to form a ⅝"-wide handle.

Hand-stitch handle onto bag sides at top outside edges.

Slip lace-trimmed ribbon onto bag, aligning ribbon with top edge of bag. Stitch in place.

Cut off zipper-pull tab from zipper pull *(if applicable.)* Slip a piece of lace through zipper pull and knot ends together.

There is a wide variety of collectibles that can be used to embellish any piece of clothing or home accessory. Vintage buttons can be strung from delicate threads and attached to a crocheted necklace, small shells collected on the beach can be stitched to the lacey sides of a box or glued to a delicate doily on the boxtop.

Tip: Vintage buttons can be purchased in antique stores that specialize in fabrics, beads, or buttons; or they can be rescued from a grandmother's button box or an old prom dress that has been gently hidden away in the cedar chest.

MATERIALS

(For 3" box)

Beads: 8mm, leaf-shaped, olive green (5)

Brocade: silk-satin, sage (¼ yd)

Crescent board

Papier-mâché box: 3", heart-shaped

Poster board

Quilt batting

Ribbons:

    1", silk-satin, natural white (2 yds)

    4mm, silk,(1 yd ea)

        bright coral; light red

        white (½ yd)

    7mm, silk, olive green (1½ yds)

Velvet: cross-dyed, coral (⅛ yd)

TOOLS

Clean cloth

Disposable paint roller: 3"

Double-stick tape

Embroidery needle: size 3

Fabric scissors

Large paper bag

Pencil

Small paint tray

Tacky glue

Tape measure

Sweetheart Treasure Box

One can never have too many pretty boxes to hold treasured items. Hearts are sentimental symbols of affection. When a box is shaped like a heart, it has practical beauty.

HOW TO MAKE THE HEART

1. Trace box opening onto crescent board. Cut out and label Lid. Trace Lid onto crescent board adding ⅛" all around. Cut out and label Middle Lid. Trace Lid onto crescent board subtracting ⅛" all around. Cut out and label Inside Lid. Cut out three more Inside Lids.

2. Glue four Inside Lids together. Cover box, Middle Lid, and Inside Lid with brocade, using your preferred method. See Step 1 on page 108 to cover inside of box with brocade.

3. Cut brocade for the Lid 1" larger all around than the Lid. Referring to the Ribbon Embroidery Diagram, embroider Lid fabric.

Ribbon Embroidery Diagram

4. Work Knotted-Loop Petal Stitches on the outer and inner circles, as well as the circle center. Bring needle up at A and tie a small knot ⅜" from entry. Form a small loop and go down at B, piercing the ribbon. Completed Knotted-Loop Petal Stitch. See (1).

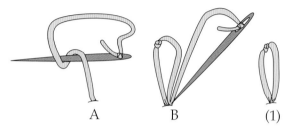

Knotted-Loop Petal Stitch

5. Work Ribbon Stitches for long leaves. Come up through fabric at A. Lay ribbon flat on fabric. At the end of the stitch, pierce the ribbon with the needle. Slowly pull the length of ribbon through, allowing ends of the ribbon to curl. See (1). Completed Ribbon Stitch. See (2).

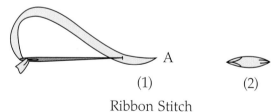

Ribbon Stitch

6. Cover work surface with the paper bag.

7. Glue a trimmed batting piece onto one side of lid and tightly wrap embroidered fabric around padded lid. Stitch leaf-shaped beads around flower.

8. Glue Middle Lid onto Inside Lid, wrong sides facing. Referring to Fluting Diagram and using double-stick tape, flute 7mm ribbon onto wrong-side edge of padded lid. Glue Lid onto Middle Lid, wrong sides together.

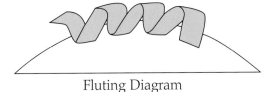

Fluting Diagram

Make Leaf

9. Cut eighteen 3½" lengths from silk-satin ribbon.

10. Fold ends of each length diagonally. See (1). Fold again.

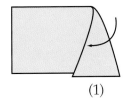

(1)

11. Gather-stitch across bottom edge of folds. Trim excess ribbon. See (2).

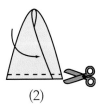

(2)

12. Gather tightly and secure thread. Completed Folded Leaf. See (3).

(3)

13. Tie remaining silk-satin ribbon into a soft bow.

14. Glue leaves onto bottom edge of box, along with bow.

Tips: An important styling consideration for your beautiful box is to make certain the inside is as exquisitely crafted as the top and outside. Tuft or line with a silky or velvety fabric.

Coordinate edging and details with ribbons, beads, and buttons.

MATERIALS

Dowels: ⅛" (4)

Matching thread

Polyester stuffing

Ribbons:

    ¼", double-faced satin, ivory (½ yd)

    ⅝", double-faced satin, light yellow (6")

    4mm, silk, pale yellow (10 yds)

Wool felt: ivory, 5" x 10"

TOOLS

Embroidery needle: size 3

Fabric scissors

Sewing machine

Straight pins

Tacky glue

Tape measure

Ribbon Fleece Lamb

The delight of this adorable little lamb is achieved with loops of ribbon stitched on in rows after the soft body is constructed.

HOW TO MAKE THE LAMB

1. Cut two pieces from felt, using Lamb Pattern.

2. Sew pieces together, taking a scant ⅛" seam allowance. Leave a 2" opening along the body but do not turn right side out.

3. Stuff lamb through opening.

4. Glue the dowels, in sets of two, into belly at each end of opening, extending dowels 1" from the opening. Let dry. Hand-stitch opening closed.

Tip: Miniature music boxes can be placed inside, with a small buttonhole made on the back of the lamb, so that a lullaby can be played to soothe an infant or a small child.

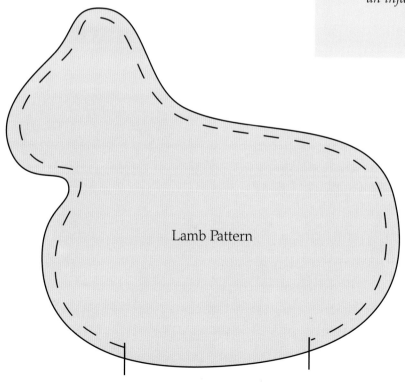

Lamb Pattern

5. Working with 18" lengths of silk ribbon, thread the ribbon through needle eye.

6. Beginning at one end along belly, stitch ribbon into felt. Ribbon knot will be covered by looped stitches.

7. Work Loop Petal Stitches with ribbon. Bring needle up. Form a small loop and go down at A, piercing ribbon. Completed Loop Petal Stitch. See (1).

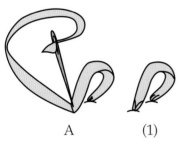

A   (1)

Loop Petal Stitch

8. Cover the entire surface of the lamb's body, working stitches directly next to each other in horizontal lines ⅜" apart. Do not embroider face or neck.

9. Tie the ivory satin ribbon around the lamb's neck.

10. Cut 1" from yellow satin ribbon and set aside. Mark center of remaining length.

11. Twist and fold one end forward diagonally to center. Pin in place. Repeat with other end. See (2).

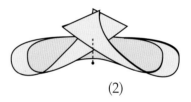

(2)

12. Hand-stitch across center through all layers.

13. Tightly pull threads to gather, then secure thread.

14. Wrap center with 1" piece of yellow ribbon and hand-stitch in place. Stitch the ears onto the top of the head.

MATERIALS

Beads:

    11/0 seed:

        crystal pink

        white

    4mm faceted rondelle:

        clear (14)

        pink (3)

    5mm x 8mm teardrop, crystal (6)

    frosted tulip, white (18)

Button: 1½", glass

Crescent board: 4" x 7"

Embroidery floss: white

Interfacing: heavy-weight nonwoven, fusible (½ yd)

Matching thread

Ribbons: ¼", double-faced silk-satin (20 yds ea)

    light-shell pink;`shell pink

    white (10⅛ yds)

Sequins: iridescent (2 yds)

Silk dupioni:

    pale pink (¼ yd)   white (¼ yd)

Wire: 32-gauge, white (18")

TOOLS

Adjustable-length doll-hair maker

Fabric-marking pen: fine tip

Grid-lined ruler

Hand-sewing needle

Iron and ironing board

Scissors: craft,fabric

Sewing machine

Straight pins

Tacky glue

Wire cutters

Perfect Little Evening Purse

Elegant and detailed with ribbons and beads, this evening purse recalls the vintage 1920s in style. The shimmer of iridescent beads on the handle and the looped fringe effects of the purse itself have flair worthy of a dancing flapper.

HOW TO MAKE THE PURSE

1. Using fabric scissors and outside oval of Purse Bottom Pattern, cut one purse bottom, five 1⅞" x 15" body strips, and one 2½" x 15" top-binding strip from white silk.

2. From pink silk, cut one 6¾" x 15" lining piece and one purse bottom lining piece, using outside oval.

3. From the interfacing, cut ten ⅜" x 7½" ribbon-fringe strips, five 1⅞" x 15" body strips, and one purse bottom, using the outside oval.

4. Fuse interfacing body strips and purse bottom onto the wrong sides of matching white silk pieces.

5. Fold each interfaced strip in half, right sides facing, aligning short ends.

6. Sew short ends together, using ½" seam allowance. Press seam allowances open.

7. Turn strips right side out. Quarter-mark top and bottom edges of each strip as well as purse bottom.

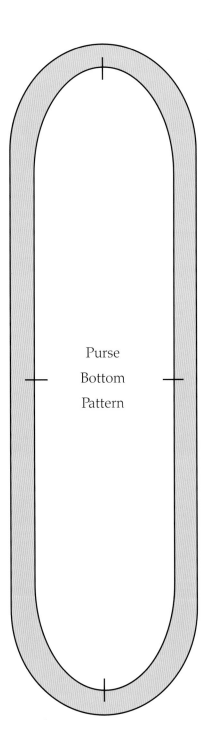

Purse

Bottom

Pattern

8. Sew one interfaced strip onto white purse bottom, right sides facing, aligning the marks and using a ¼" seam allowance. Press the seam allowance open.

9. From right side, fold along seam line and topstitch the layers together close to seam.

Make Ribbon Fringe

10. Set doll-hair maker with a 2½" space between parallel bars. Tape one end of a 5-yd length of shell-pink ribbon onto one bar end.

11. Extend ribbon to the parallel bar and wrap it snugly around bar, twisting ribbon two times. Extend ribbon back up, around, and over beginning bar. Continue to wrap ribbon around bars in this manner for 7". Tape remaining ribbon end to beginning bar. See (1).

12. Hand-stitch a ⅜"-wide interfacing strip over the wrapped ribbon 1¾" up from the lower parallel bar. See (2).

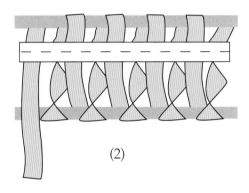

(2)

13. Cut wrapped ribbon from bars above interfacing strip. See (3). Repeat this process to make ribbon fringe: three more lengths from shell-pink fringe, four from light-shell-pink fringe, and two from white fringe. *Note: Each fringed row on purse will use two fringed pieces of ribbon.*

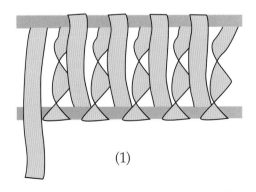

(1)

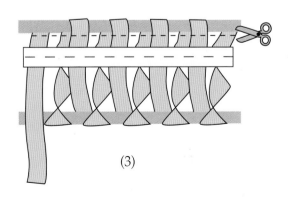

(3)

14. Pin interfaced edges of two shell-pink fringe pieces onto upper edge of first body strip attached in Step 4. Machine-baste fringe in place. See (4).

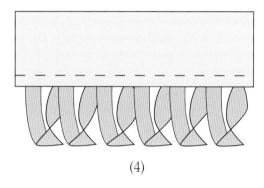

(4)

15. Sew a second body strip from Step 3 onto top edge of first strip, right sides facing, matching quarter marks and using a ¼" seam allowance. Finger-press seam allowance toward upper strip and topstitch close to seam. Hand-stitch sequins onto seam line.

16. Repeat Step 7 to machine-baste the cut edges of two lengths of the light-shell-pink fringe to upper edge of second strip. Repeat Step 8.

17. Repeat Steps 9–10 to sew another row of shell-pink fringe onto body. Repeat Steps 5–6 to sew another row of light-shell-pink fringe onto body. Baste-stitch white fringe onto upper edge of final strip.

18. Using craft scissors and inside oval of Purse Bottom Pattern page 100, cut and glue together two pieces from crescent board. Glue pieces onto inside purse bottom.

19. Fold the body lining in half, right sides facing, aligning 6¾" edges. Sew, using ½" seam allowance. Quarter-mark the top and bottom edges and purse bottom lining. Sew the lining pieces together, right sides facing, matching the quarter marks. Press the seam allowance open.

20. Slip lining inside purse, aligning top edges.

21. Cut a 4" length from white ribbon. Loop ribbon and align the cut ends with the top outside edge of purse at center quarter-mark and pin.

22. Fold top binding strip in half, aligning 2½" ends. Sew ends, using ½" seam allowance. Sew one long edge of strip to top purse edge, right sides facing, using ¼" seam allowance. Press and fold strip over to inside. Turn raw edge under ½", then under again to enclose seam and hand-stitch in place.

Tip: For the handle of your new evening bag, use a necklace. If necessary, re-string the necklace to ensure the strength of the handle.

Tip: A purse this size is perfect for an evening bag. Made larger in brightly printed ribbons, it is ideal for a day of shopping or one spent at the beach.

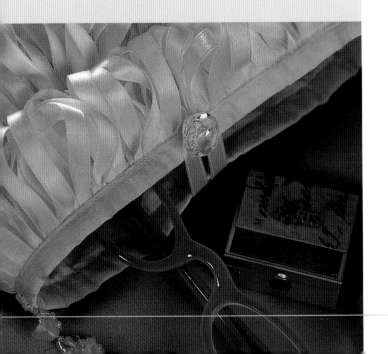

23. Arrange and slip beads onto an 18" length of wire. Once beaded, coil ends and hand-stitch coil onto outside ends of purse with embroidery floss.

24. Hand-stitch glass button onto top-binding strip at center front of purse.

MATERIALS

Blank cards: 3" x 5" (6)

Button(s): (1 large or 5 small per card)

Decorative vellum and specialty papers

Ribbons: silk, (½ yd ea)

    ¼"; ⅝"; 1½"; 4mm

TOOLS

Craft scissors

Glue stick

Hand-sewing needle

Handmade Cards

HOW TO MAKE THE CARDS

1. Trim a piece of vellum or specialty paper to decorate card front and glue in place as desired.

2. Stitch one or more buttons onto cards with silk ribbon.

3. Cut a piece of paper the same size as card and glue in place over stitching inside card.

Pretty papers and ribbon make the most ordinary cards quite elegant. Card giving is always more special when the card is handcrafted. Begin with good quality card stock. Enhance with papers, ribbons, and buttons.

MATERIALS

Beads:

   11/0, seed, pearlescent colors

   3mm pearl, white (10–50)

   4mm rondelle, rhinestone (10–50)

   5mm, frosted white (10–50)

   6mm round, flat, orchid (10–50)

   faceted, lavender (10–50)

Crescent board

Handmade papers:

   purple variegated

   off-white

Matching thread

Papier-mâché box: 3", round

Poster board

Quilt batting: 3" scrap

Ribbon: 7mm, hand-dyed silk, lavender (6 yds)

Silk dupioni: pale lavender (5" scrap)

Vintage velvet flowers: off-white (3)

Wire: 26-gauge, silver or white (6")

TOOLS

Clean rag	Scissors:
Foam paintbrush	craft
Large paper bag	fabric
Needles:	Small glue tray
beading	Straight pins
darning	Tacky glue
Pencil	Tape measure
Ruler	

Delicate Scalloped Box

From a simple concept of covering a box with rows of satin ribbon, this container idea has exquisite details. The scalloped border design of the box-top creates a pleasing rhythm with low points evenly spaced for bead dangles.

1. Cover work surface with paper bag. Using tape measure and craft scissors, measure and cut purple variegated paper to cover inside of box. Glue paper in place.

2. Measure and cut poster board ½" taller than outside of box and so that it wraps around box with a 1" overlap.

3. Using 1½" Template, trace scallops along one long edge of the poster board.

1½" Template

4. Cut two 1" x 11" strips from off-white paper. Glue strips onto front and back of scalloped edge of poster board. Trim around scallops. Wrap and glue poster board around box.

5. Beginning at 1" overlap, glue one end of ribbon to upper edge just below a scallop dip. Continuously wrap ribbon downward around box, overlapping ribbon a scant 1/16" and periodically gluing ribbon onto box side. Glue remaining ribbon end onto box bottom.

6. Cut new base for box from crescent board ⅛" larger than box bottom.

7. Cover new box bottom with off-white paper and glue onto box bottom, wrong sides together.

8. Thread beading needle with doubled thread, allowing looped thread end to be longer than cut ends. Begin stitching at a scallop dip and stitch through thread loop, invisibly knotting thread onto box.

9. Slide three specialty beads onto thread alternating each with a seed bead. Plan for a seed bead as the first and last bead. Stitch around last seed bead and back through beads in opposite direction. See (1).

(1)

10. Stitch thread into box while pulling beads up to meet scallop dip. Knot thread 2–3 times, then slip thread back through beads and trim off excess. Repeat for each scallop dip.

11. Using beading needle and thread, encircle top of new base with beads, arranging beads in a pleasing fashion.

12. Cut new Lid from crescent board that fits just within box. Using craft scissors, cut four Inside Lids from crescent board ⅛" smaller all around than Lid.

13. Using fabric scissors and Lid as a template, cut a circle from silk fabric ¾" larger all around than Lid.

14. Glue quilt batting onto top of Lid and trim excess.

15. Cover padded Lid with silk fabric and glue edges in place on back side of cardboard.

16. Glue Inside Lids together.

17. Using the glued Inside Lid as a template, cut a circle from purple paper ¾" larger than Inside Lid.

18. Cover the Inside Lid and glue the paper in place.

19. Bead 3" of 6" length of wire, using seed beads between specialty beads at center. Position beads at center of wire. Bend wire to form a loop and twist ends together for the handle.

20. Puncture a hole through the center top of the Lid, using darning needle.

21. Slip the wire ends through the hole and tape or glue wires onto the underside of Lid to anchor the handle.

22. Glue Inside Lid onto Lid, wrong sides together.

23. Glue velvet flowers onto the Lid for desired embellishment.

MATERIALS

Beads: coordinate colors with fabric and garland

    11/0 seed

    4mm round (10–30)

    6mm round (10–30)

    various-sized specialty shapes (10–30)

Fabric or paper to cover lamp shade

Neutral thread

Self-adhesive lamp shade: small

Trim: rosebud (¾ yd)

TOOLS

Beading needle

Fabric-marking pen: fine tip

Large paper bag

Pinking shears

Scissors:

    craft

    fabric

Tacky glue

Bead & Garland Lamp Shade

These bead-draped and rose-bordered lamp shades are easier to make than they look, thanks to garland trims. The challenge will be in deciding which beautiful colors of paper, rosebuds, and beads to use in each room.

HOW TO MAKE THE LAMP SHADE

Cover work surface. Refer to manu-facturer's directions for covering self-adhesive lamp shade. Cut fabric or paper according to directions and adhere onto lamp shade.

Using pinking shears, trim excess fabric along top and bottom edges. Glue excess fabric onto inside of lamp shade with tacky glue.

Section and mark top and/or bottom edges of lamp shade into halves, thirds, or quarters, depending on how lamp shade will be draped with beads and garland.

Slip doubled thread through needle eye. Align ends and knot, so thread is quadrupled.

Stitch thread into top edge of lamp shade at mark. Slip beads onto thread in a pleasing arrangement to create a bead drape, alternating one seed bead with each larger bead.

When satisfied with length of bead drape, stitch thread into top edge of lamp shade at next mark, securing thread.

Continue to slip beads onto thread to create bead drapes, anchoring each drape at top edge of lamp shade. Trim excess thread.

Glue the rosebud garland onto the top or bottom edges, or vertically onto lamp shade.

By looking at the four lamp shades on these pages, you can see how one lamp base can look different according to the chosen shade styling.

MATERIALS

Beads:

    4mm, round (7)

    5mm, gold-tipped beads (24)

    tulip-shaped, plum (3)

Braid: ⅛", plum (1⅝ yds)

Embroidery floss: purple

Matching thread

Purse frame: 2¾", brass

Ribbon garland: buds and bows, plum/green (¼ yd)

Ribbons:

    4mm, silk, (1–3 yds ea) dark blue; purple

    21mm, ruffled satin, plum (2 yds)

    25mm, satin-edged crepe georgette, dark plum (1 yd)

Silk fabric: black (8½" x 13")

Wire-edged ribbons: taffeta

    15mm, brown/blue (1 yd)

    25mm, copper (1½ yds)

TOOLS

Fabric-marking pen: fine tip

Fabric scissors

Iron and ironing board

Needles:

    beading

    hand-sewing

Sewing machine

Tacky glue

Tape measure

Bridesmaid's Ribbon Purse

HOW TO MAKE THE PURSE

1. Cut four 14" lengths from ruffled satin ribbon and two 14" lengths from crepe georgette ribbon.

2. Cut three 14" lengths from copper taffeta ribbon. Remove wire from both selvages.

3. Invisibly hand-stitch ribbon lengths together, overlapping ruffled satin onto selvages of ribbons in following order, working left to right: taffeta, ruffled satin, crepe georgette, ruffled satin, taffeta, ruffled satin, crepe georgette, ruffled satin, taffeta to create a piece of vertically striped ribbons. See (1).

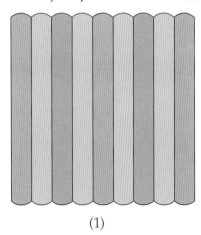

(1)

4. Press ribbons flat from wrong side. Trim top and bottom edges of ribbon piece so they are clean and straight, measuring 13" long.

5. Using an embroidery needle with the blue and purple silk ribbons and beginning 2" down from the top edge of the piece, embroider a 2"-long spray of Bullion Lazy-daisy Stitches along each length of copper taffeta stripes. Come up at A. Go down at B. Wrap loop around needle. Go down at B. Completed stitch. See (2).

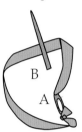

(2)

Bullion Lazy-daisy Stitch

6. Fold piece in half, wrong sides facing and aligning top and bottom edges. Using hand-sewing needle with matching thread and beginning 1¾" down from top edge, whipstitch sides together.

7. Cut two 18" lengths from brown/blue wired taffeta ribbon. Remove wire from only one edge of each length.

8. Working with one length, fold ribbon in half, aligning cut ends. Using embroidery needle with two strands of purple embroidery floss, whipstitch together selvages with wire removed. See (3). Repeat with second length.

(3)

9. Working with one length of whip-stitched ribbon, pull wire ends so ribbon gathers along remaining edge to 4¾" length. Twist wire ends together and trim excess wire. Repeat with second length.

10. Fold cut end in ¼" to inside of ribbon and hand-stitch together.

11. Beginning 2" down from top edge of pocket, whipstitch wired edge of one gathered ribbon to stitched edge of purse. See (4). Repeat with second length of ribbon on remaining side.

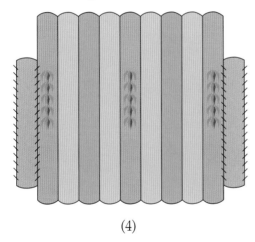

(4)

12. Fold silk fabric in half, right sides facing and aligning 8½" edges. Beginning 2" down from top edges, sew sides, using a ¼" seam allowance. Press seam allowances open, including upper 2" along seam line. Slip lining into purse.

13. Gather-stitch along top front edge of purse, through layers, using ½" seam allowance.

14. Pull gathering thread to match width of purse frame and knot thread. Hand-stitch gathered edge onto inside of purse frame through frame holes.

15. Repeat with back top edge. Allow the purse sides to fall outward over the frame.

16. Trim top edges to a scant ¼" seam allowance. Glue the garland over the edges.

17. Close purse and mark bottom folded edge. Gather-stitch across folded edge. Pull gathers as tightly as possible and secure thread.

18. Hand-stitch gold-tipped beads onto purse frame front and back. Stitch bead dangles onto gathered bottom edge.

19. Slip one end of braid through both purse frame handle loops.

20. Align braid ends and stitch together, then wrap and stitch a scrap of ribbon around center of braid handle.

MATERIALS

Beads:

    round, pale pink (30)

    seed, fuchsia

    short bugles, crystal

    stars, pale pink (12)

    teardrop, crystal (10)

    tube, pink (14)

    tulip, frosted white (6)

Burn-out chiffon with velvet: variegated pink (⅓ yd)

Matching thread

Ribbon: ¾", silk-satin, pink (⅔ yd)

TOOLS

Fabric scissors

Iron and ironing board

Needle: fine embroidery or beading

Sewing machine

Straight pins

Tape measure

Brilliant Beaded Scarf

A sheer scarf is more dramatic when the color is brilliant. Add bead trim on the edges and perhaps here and there on the scarf for a stunning complement to a black or white outfit.

1. Fold chiffon in half lengthwise and trim to square up all edges.

2. Cut the ribbon in half. Pin outside edge of one ribbon length ½" in from each end of fabric, right sides up.

3. Sew both edges of ribbon lengths onto fabric, using matching thread. Press from back side of fabric.

4. Fold chiffon in half lengthwise, right sides facing, aligning the long edges.

5. Sew the long edges together, using ½" seam allowance and leaving 3" opening near center of seam. See (1). Press the seam allowance open.

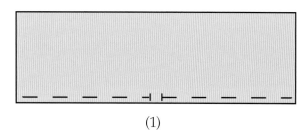

(1)

6. With right sides facing, position seam so it is centered between long edges. See (2).

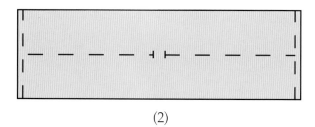

(2)

7. Pin in place and sew across each end, along outside edge of ribbon.

8. Trim bulk from corners and turn scarf right side out through center seam opening. Press ends lightly.

9. Using a seed bead between each specialty bead, hand-stitch dangles at ½" intervals to form beaded fringe at scarf ends. Refer to page 108 for dangle instructions.

Tip: If you do not want to do your own beading, beautifully beaded trims can be purchased for a reasonable price at most fabric stores.

Beautiful beaded scarves are usually worn only on very special occasions, then gently tucked away in a drawer. To enjoy them daily, try draping them over a dresser top or an open door. They also look beautiful hung on top of towels in a powder room, or if large enough, laid across the foot of the bed in a guest room.

MATERIALS

Child's shoe: size 5

Matching thread

Polyester stuffing

Poster board: white (5" x 7½")

Ribbons:

    1½", embroidered (¼ yd)

    2mm, silk, brown (½ yd)

    4mm, silk, black (1 yd)

    7mm, silk, black (1 yd)

    25mm, taffeta, olive green (⅓ yd)

Silk dupioni: burnished gold (¼ yd)

Trim: rosebud, ¼" (¼ yd)

Velvet: cross-dyed, burgundy/olive (¼ yd)

TOOLS

Disposable paint roller: 3"

Double-stick tape

Dowel

Embroidery needle

Hot-glue gun and glue sticks

Large paper bag

Paint tray

Pencil

Scissors:

    craft

    fabric

Tacky glue

Tape measure

Exotic Shoe Pincushion

This little shoe pincushion could have stepped straight from Tales of the Arabian Nights. The charm of its diminutive size and exotic fabrics invite embellishment with trims, beads, and, of course, pins.

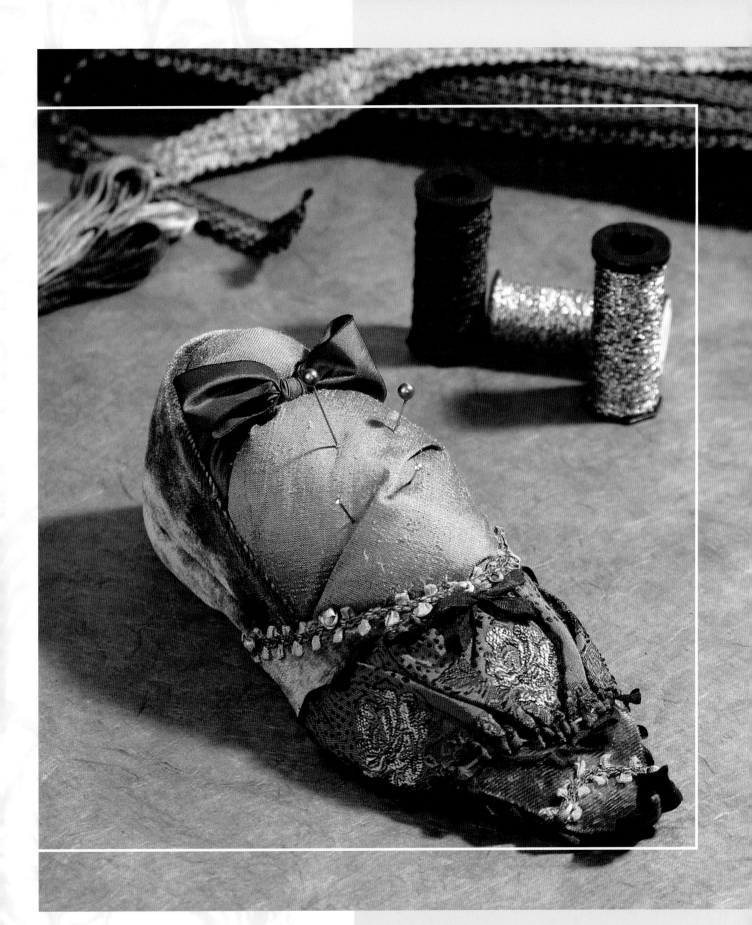

HOW TO MAKE THE PINCUSHION

1. Cover work surface. From poster board, cut one Vamp, one Sole, and one Oval using patterns on page 125. *Note: Adjust pattern to fit shoe as needed.*

2. From bias of velvet, cut one 9" x 3" strip. From remaining velvet, cut one piece for Vamp and Sole ½" larger all around. From silk fabric, cut one Oval, using poster-board template.

3. Place poster-board Vamp over shoe toe and mark at shoe sides. *Note: Toe tip is more pointed than on actual shoe.*

4. Using tacky glue, laminate bias strip onto shoe sides and back. Overlap side markings 1". Wrap and glue excess fabric to underside and inside of shoe. Using fingernail, press in along top of heel to define.

5. Laminate velvet pieces onto Vamp and Sole. Wrap and glue fabric edges to wrong sides, clipping and trimming bulk.

6. Using a dowel, roll Vamp sides to fit curves of shoe top. Hot-glue Vamp in place. *Note: Toe portion of Vamp will not fit snugly over shoe.*

7. Cut 2mm ribbon in half. Using embroidery needle and one length 2mm ribbon, gather-stitch along each selvage edge of 1½" ribbon.

8. Position 1½" ribbon across top of Vamp, gathering both selvages to fit. Glue in place.

9. Cut 4mm ribbon in half. Tie small bow at each ribbon center. Glue one bow onto center top selvage edge of 1½" ribbon trim.

10. Cascade-stitch ribbon tails along upper edge of trim. See Cascade Stitch on page 39. Repeat at trim's bottom edge.

11. Glue pieces of rosebud trim near tip and along upper edge of Vamp.

12. Using double-stick tape, Flute 7mm ribbon onto underside of Vamp. See fluting on page 93. Extend ribbon ⅛" past edge.

13. Hot-glue Sole onto the bottom of shoe, aligning tips. Using the pencil, curl tip.

14. Gather-stitch outer edge of silk oval to form a cup.

15. Fill cup firmly with polyester stuffing. Tightly pull gathers and secure for pincushion.

16. Tie bow at center of 25mm ribbon and glue onto pincushion top.

17. Extend ribbon ends around pincushion and hot-glue onto underside. Glue pincushion inside shoe.

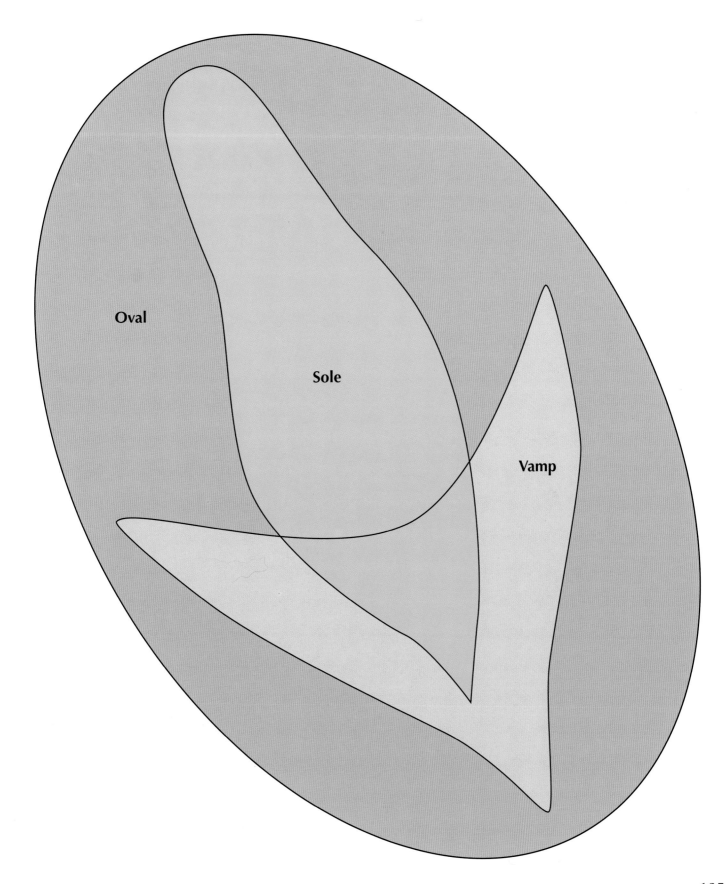

Oval

Sole

Vamp

Acknowledgements

The author would like to thank the following suppliers for the use of their products.

Accu Cut
1035 E. Dodge Street
Fremont, NE 68025
800-288-1670
Die-cut Boxes
Page 8

Anna Griffin Incorporated
733 Lambert Drive
Atlanta, GA 30324
404-817-8170
www.annagriffin.com
Specialty Papers
Pages 66, 104

Bag Lady Press
P.O. Box 2409
Evergreen, CO 80437-2409
303-670-2177
www.baglady.com
Brass Purse Frame
Page 114

Blue Moon Beads
4218 Howard Avenue
Kensington, MD 20895
310-897-8311
www.bluemoonbeads.com
Beads
Pages 106, 110, 114

Hanah Silk, from Artemis
179 High Street
So. Portland, ME 04106
www.artemisinc.com/wholesale
Bias Cut Ribbon
Pages 50, 70

Lina G's
468 Morro Bay Blvd.
Morro Bay, CA 93442
805-772-7759
www.trimsandribbons.com
Vintage Flowers
Pages 8, 106

Marcel Schurman Co.
Division of Schurman Fine
    Papers
500 Chadbourne Road
Box 6030
Fairfield, CA 94533
800-333-6724
Decorative Tissue Paper
Page 8

Mokuba
55 West 39th Street
New York, NY 10018
212-869-8900
Ribbons
*Pages 8, 26, 46, 66, 70, 78,
    114, 122*

Provo Craft
151 East 3450 North
Spanish Fork, UT 84660
800-937-7686
www.provocraft.com
Glass Ovals
Page 34

Quilter's Resource
P.O. Box 148850
Chicago, IL 60614
800-676-6543
www.quiltersresource.com
Ribbons
Pages 66, 114

Ruban et Fleur
7664 Melrose Avenue
Los Angeles, CA 90046
323-653-2227
www.rubanetfleur.com
Vintage Flowers and Ribbon
Pages 8, 66

YLI Corporation
161 W. Main Street
Rock Hill, SC 29730
803-985-3100
www.ylicorp.com
Ribbons
Pages 106, 114

Metric Conversion Chart

mm-millimetres cm-centimetres
inches to millimetres and centimetres

inches	mm	cm	inches	cm	inches	cm
1/8	3	0.3	9	22.9	30	76.2
1/4	6	0.6	10	25.4	31	78.7
1/2	13	1.3	12	30.5	33	83.8
5/8	16	1.6	13	33.0	34	86.4
3/4	19	1.9	14	35.6	35	88.9
7/8	22	2.2	15	38.1	36	91.4
1	25	2.5	16	40.6	37	94.0
1 1/4	32	3.2	17	43.2	38	96.5
1 1/2	38	3.8	18	45.7	39	99.1
1 3/4	44	4.4	19	48.3	40	101.6
2	51	5.1	20	50.8	41	104.1
2 1/2	64	6.4	21	53.3	42	106.7
3	76	7.6	22	55.9	43	109.2
3 1/2	89	8.9	23	58.4	44	111.8
4	102	10.2	24	61.0	45	114.3
4 1/2	114	11.4	25	63.5	46	116.8
5	127	12.7	26	66.0	47	119.4
6	152	15.2	27	68.6	48	121.9
7	178	17.8	28	71.1	49	124.5
8	203	20.3	29	73.7	50	127.0

yards to metres

yards	metres	yards	metres	yards	metres	yards	metres	yards	metres
1/8	0.11	2 1/8	1.94	4 1/8	3.77	6 1/8	5.60	8 1/8	7.43
1/4	0.23	2 1/4	2.06	4 1/4	3.89	6 1/4	5.72	8 1/4	7.54
3/8	0.34	2 3/8	2.17	4 3/8	4.00	6 3/8	5.83	8 3/8	7.66
1/2	0.46	2 1/2	2.29	4 1/2	4.11	6 1/2	5.94	8 1/2	7.77
5/8	0.57	2 5/8	2.40	4 5/8	4.23	6 5/8	6.06	8 5/8	7.89
3/4	0.69	2 3/4	2.51	4 3/4	4.34	6 3/4	6.17	8 3/4	8.00
7/8	0.80	2 7/8	2.63	4 7/8	4.46	6 7/8	6.29	8 7/8	8.12
1	0.91	3	2.74	5	4.57	7	6.40	9	8.23
1 1/8	1.03	3 1/8	2.86	5 1/8	4.69	7 1/8	6.52	9 1/8	8.34
1 1/4	1.14	3 1/4	2.97	5 1/4	4.80	7 1/4	6.63	9 1/4	8.46
1 3/8	1.26	3 3/8	3.09	5 3/8	4.91	7 3/8	6.74	9 3/8	8.57
1 1/2	1.37	3 1/2	3.20	5 1/2	5.03	7 1/2	6.86	9 1/2	8.69
1 5/8	1.49	3 5/8	3.31	5 5/8	5.14	7 5/8	6.97	9 5/8	8.80
1 3/4	1.60	3 3/4	3.43	5 3/4	5.26	7 3/4	7.09	9 3/4	8.92
1 7/8	1.71	3 7/8	3.54	5 7/8	5.37	7 7/8	7.20	9 7/8	9.03
2	1.83	4	3.66	6	5.49	8	7.32	10	9.14

Index

Make Petal

1. Cut eleven 4" lengths of the taffeta ribbon.

2. Fold one length of ribbon in half, matching cut ends.

3. At fold, fold corners down ¼" toward back of petal. Glue folds in place. See (1).

(1)

4. Repeat Steps 2–3 for remaining ribbon lengths.

5. Stitch a deep pleat at cut ends so petal will cup. See (2). Repeat for all petals.

Above: This adorable baby doll in a blue bunny suit has had bunny ears stitched down to suggest a bonnet with a bow.

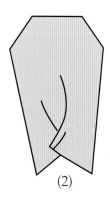

(2)

At a baby shower, have each guest autograph the baby with good wishes. The expectant mother will treasure this personalized keepsake.

Make Collar

6. Gather-stitch petals together in a chain, placing stitches ¼" in from cut edges.

7. Position petal-chain collar at doll's neck and join the last petal to the first.

8. Tightly pull gathering stitches so collar fits snugly. Secure stitches and knot thread.

Embellish Doll

9. Stitch star-shaped beads onto doll's clothing for buttons.

10. Tie silk-satin ribbon into a soft bow around doll's head and knot ends.

Tip: Use a fine embroidery needle rather than a beading needle to sew beads and buttons onto fabrics.

MATERIALS

(For 2" x 3" frame opening)

Assorted buttons: sizes ¼"–¾", pink; white (25)

Metal photograph frame

Ribbon: 4mm, silk, pale pink (12")

TOOLS

E-6000 adhesive

Large paper bag

Tape measure

Toothpick

Beautiful Buttons Frame

HOW TO EMBELLISH THE FRAME

1. Cover the work surface with paper bag.

2. Arrange 2–3 layers of buttons around outer edge of opening. Using toothpick, adhere in place.

3. Before placing the last button, tie silk ribbon into a small bow and adhere in place near bottom of frame.

4. Adhere last button over knot of bow.

Marble-like bright buttons sparkle up the art of framing loved ones. Sort all buttons by color and pattern keyed to the decor where the frame will be displayed to make it a one-of-a-kind.